A ROOKIE BIOGRAPHY

MARY McLEOD BETHUNE

Champion for Education

By Carol Greene

CHILDRENS PRESS®
CHICAGO

Mary McLeod Bethune (1875-1955)

Library of Congress Cataloging-in-Publication Data

Greene, Carol.
   Mary McLeod Bethune : champion for education / by Carol Greene.
     p. cm. — (A Rookie biography)
   Summary: Simple text traces the life and achievements of the black
educator who was instrumental in creating opportunities for blacks in
education and government.
   ISBN 0-516-04255-6
   1. Bethune, Mary McLeod, 1875-1955—Juvenile literature. 2. Afro-
Americans—Biography—Juvenile literature. 3. Teachers—United
States—Biography—Juvenile literature. [1. Bethune, Mary McLeod, 1875-
1955. 2. Teachers. 3. Afro-Americans—Biography.] I. Title. II. Series:
Greene, Carol. Rookie biography.
E185.97.B34G72   1993
370′.92—dc20
  [B]   92-37013
                                                CIP
                                                 AC

Mary McLeod Bethune
was a real person.
She was born in 1875.
She died in 1955.
Mrs. Bethune helped
many black children
get a good education.
This is her story.

TABLE OF CONTENTS

Mary was born in this house in Mayesville, South Carolina.

Chapter 1

Different

‡‡

"She is different . . . special,"
said Mary's mother.

"This is a different one,"
said her Grandma Sophia.

But baby Mary Jane McLeod
just lay there, fast asleep.

She was the fifteenth child
of Patsy and Samuel McLeod.
She was also the first one
in her family
to be born a free person.

President Abraham Lincoln (third from left) signed the
Emancipation Proclamation that set the slaves free.

The McLeods had been
slaves all their lives.
Their older children
had been slaves, too.

Then, in 1863,
President Abraham Lincoln
set the slaves free.

The McLeods worked hard
to buy a tiny farm near
Mayesville, South Carolina.
They were very poor.
But now they could hope
for a better life.

They believed that God
had sent Mary to help them
find that better life.

Mary was a good child.
But at first she didn't
do anything different.

She rode Old Bush,
the family's mule.
She took care of
the vegetable garden.
She picked cotton.

Children worked next to adults picking cotton. This was often the only way
poor families could earn money to buy the things they needed.

Then one day, Mary
was playing with
a white child.
Mary picked up a book
and pretended to read.

"Put down that book,"
said the white child.
"You can't read it."

That hurt Mary.
She *wanted* to read.
But there were no schools
for black children.

Emma J. Wilson
started the Mayesville
Industrial Institute.

Later, Mary was working
in the cotton field
with her family.
Suddenly, a woman
came toward them.

She was Miss Emma J. Wilson.
A church had sent her
to start a school
for black children.

Mary's parents, Samuel and Patsy McLeod

Mary's parents quickly
made up their minds.
Mary must go to that school.

So one October day,
Mary walked to Mayesville
and started school.
It was a poor little school.
But Mary didn't care.
She was learning to read.

At last she told her family,
"I can read!"
And she picked up a Bible
and read to them.

"Praise God!" cried her parents
and Grandma Sophia.
They had been right.
Mary *was* different.

Most of the freed slaves could not read because
they had never been allowed to go to school.

Chapter 2

Away from Home

Mary learned many things
at Miss Wilson's school.
She even used her math
to help her father get
a fair price for his cotton.

After four years,
Mary graduated.
Now she wanted to go
to Scotia Seminary
in Concord, North Carolina.
But that cost money.

"I'll pay for her to go
to that school somehow,"
said Samuel McLeod.

Then the family's mule died.
They had to use their money
to buy a new one.

Everyone felt terrible.
But Mary asked God to help
her go to the school.

One day, Miss Wilson
ran up to the door.

"Mary!" she cried.
"You're going to
Scotia after all!"

A woman in Colorado,
Mary Crissman,
earned her living
making dresses.

Mrs. Crissman didn't
have much money.
But she gave what she had
as a scholarship
for one black child.
Mary McLeod won it.

"It's a miracle!" said Mary.

Her new school looked
like a miracle, too.
It was big and beautiful.

Education was important. Eager to learn, the
children of former slaves attended overcrowded schools.

Mary was only twelve.
She was scared.
But she stayed.

Soon Mary loved
her new life.
As time went by,
she thought she'd like
to be a missionary
in Africa someday.

So after seven years,
Mary went on to
Moody Bible Institute
in Chicago, Illinois.
Mrs. Crissman still helped her.

STUDENTS' AID SOCIETY

Of the Women's Department of

THE BIBLE INSTITUTE

For Home and Foreign Missions,

CHICAGO.

Annual Membership, - - - Two Dollars.
Life Membership, - - - Fifty Dollars.

OBJECT: to aid promising young women who lack the means to pay for board while being trained at The Bible Institute.

The selection of such women lies with the Board of Managers of the Society.

While the ordinary remuneration of Christian workers will not admit of such aid being accepted as a loan, a pledge being given for its repayment, it is felt that recipients will make such return as they can afford from time to time in contributions.

THE FUNDS are obtained by donations and membership fees.

TREASURER: MRS. ARTHUR PERCY FITT, 250 LaSalle Avenue, Chicago: to whom all contributions should be sent.

The main building of the Moody Bible Institute (above). When Mary McLeod studied there in the 1890s, she was helped by donations from the Students' Aid Society.

Mary had almost finished college when she heard some bad news. There were no openings for black missionaries in Africa.

17

Graduation picture of Mary's class at the Moody Bible Institute

Chapter 3

Rivers to Cross

Mary didn't know
what to do next.
First she went back
to Mayesville and taught
at Miss Wilson's school.

Then she taught
in Augusta, Georgia.

Mary saved enough money
to buy her parents a house
near Sumter, South Carolina.
Soon she was teaching
at a school near them.

There she met Albertus Bethune.
They got married in 1898.
A year later, their son
Albert was born.

A photo of Mary McLeod Bethune taken when she was in her twenties

But Mary couldn't stay home.
She had to be teaching.
She felt like a missionary
in her own country.
There was so much to do!

Then Mary had three dreams.
They were all about
crossing rivers.
The dreams helped Mary
know what to do next.

The first dream led her
to Palatka, Florida.
There she helped
start a school.

Mary McLeod Bethune (far right) supervised teachers at a black school located seven miles north of Daytona Beach, Florida.

The second dream made
Mary think about starting
her own school.

A friend told her
that black children
were having a hard time
in Daytona, Florida.
Mary decided to start
her school there.

Daytona was becoming a resort town when Mrs. Bethune arrived in 1903.

When Mary got to Daytona,
she had only $1.50.
But she had
her third dream, too.
It made her brave enough
to go on and try.

Mary rented a small house.
It cost $11.00 a month.
She got the money somehow.
She used wooden boxes
for desks and chairs.
Her own desk was a barrel.

On October 3, 1904,
Mary opened her school.
Five little girls came.
They felt lucky.

But Mary wasn't finished.
She had more dreams—
and more rivers to cross.

Mrs. Bethune
welcomed little
girls to her
new school
with a kind smile.

Mrs. Bethune made many phone calls to raise money for her school.

Chapter 4

More to Do

Mary's school grew quickly.
By 1905, she had 100 girls.
Many lived at the school.
Mary needed more space.

By now, Mary was good at
asking people for money.
Some hurt her feelings.
But that didn't stop her.
She cared only
about her school.

One day, Mary bought
some land that had been
a trash dump.
She hired men to clear it.

James Gamble,
John D. Rockefeller,
and Thomas H. White
(left to right) were some
of the wealthy people
who helped Mrs. Bethune.

Then she began talking
to very rich people.
Some of them listened
and some of them helped her.

In 1906, Mary's school moved
to its new building.
Mary called it Faith Hall.

Mrs. Bethune's students on the steps of Faith Hall

Most people called Mary
"Mrs. Bethune" now.
But her students
called her "Mother Dear,"
because she was like
a mother to them.

One day, one of Mary's girls
became very sick.
She needed an operation.
But the hospital didn't
want to help her
because she was black.

Mary made them take her in
and do the operation.
But the next day she found
the girl in a bed on
the hospital's back porch.

Mary was very angry.
So she started
her own hospital
right next to her school.

And the school kept growing.
Mary bought a farm.
She built new buildings.
People all across America
knew about her now.

An agriculture class at Mrs. Bethune's school in the 1930s

Above: Mary McLeod Bethune and members of the National Council of Negro Women.
Below: As Mrs. Bethune and other African-American leaders look on, President Harry S
Truman signs a document that made February 1 National Freedom Day.

She worked for the National Association for the Advancement of Colored People (NAACP). She worked for the Red Cross, too.

Mrs. Bethune walks a picket line to protest racial discrimination.

One day, Mary stood on
a stage to give a speech.
A very special person
was with her—
Mrs. Crissman.

The two women hugged
each other hard.
Without Mrs. Crissman,
Mary could not have done
the great things she did.

Mary McLeod made many speeches on
behalf of education and human rights.

White Hall (above) was named for Mrs. Bethune's
friend and supporter Thomas H. White.

Chapter 5

A Busy Woman

By 1925, Mary's school
had become a college.
It joined with another college
and Mary became president.

By 1927, the college
was doing so well that
Mary took a vacation.
She went to Europe
and had a grand time.

In 1928, a hurricane
tore Daytona apart.
Then in 1929, the Great Depression
tore all America apart.
People had no money.

But Mary was strong and wise.
She brought her college
through the hard times.

Mrs. Bethune always encouraged young women to reach for the top.

Mary McLeod Bethune and Eleanor Roosevelt became close friends. Mrs. Bethune worked with President Franklin D. Roosevelt (right) to help young black people.

Later, she helped
the president—
Franklin D. Roosevelt—
start programs for
young black people.
At last she moved
to Washington, D.C.

Mary didn't forget
her college, though.
She used much of
her pay to help it.

In 1935, the NAACP gave
Mary its Spingarn Medal.
That was a great honor.
Mary said it made her
feel stronger and braver.

The "Black Cabinet" of African-American leaders was formed
by Mrs. Bethune to deal with problems of minority groups.

**Mrs. Bethune received many awards for her
service to education and human rights.**

When Mary retired,
she moved to a house
on her college's farm.
Her students and
other young people
took care of her.

Mary's son Albert Bethune (above) attended a ceremony marking the issuance of a postage stamp in honor of his mother in 1985. More than 3,500 people attended Mrs. Bethune's funeral service at Bethune-Cookman College (below).

On her headstone, the people who loved Mary McLeod Bethune carved the message, "She has given her best that others may live a more abundant life."

Mary McLeod Bethune died on May 18, 1955. She was buried on the farm.

The stone at the foot of her grave tells how young black people felt about Mary Bethune. On it is the word: Mother.

Mrs. Bethune's faith and her Bible guided her all her life.

Important Dates

1875 July 10—Born at Mayesville, South Carolina, to Patsy and Samuel McLeod

1884 Entered Miss Emma Wilson's school

1887 Entered Scotia Seminary, Concord, North Carolina

1894 Entered Moody Bible Institute, Chicago, Illinois

1898 Married Albertus Bethune

1903 Moved to Daytona, Florida

1904 Opened Daytona Educational and Industrial School for Negro Girls (later called Daytona Normal and Industrial Institute for Girls)

1911 Opened McLeod Hospital

1935 Received NAACP's Spingarn Medal

1955 May 18—Died in Daytona, Florida

INDEX

Page numbers in boldface type indicate illustrations.

ABOUT THE AUTHOR

Carol Greene has degrees in English literature and musicology. She has worked in international exchange programs, as an editor, and as a teacher of writing. She now lives in Webster Groves, Missouri, and writes full-time. She has published more than 100 books, including those in the Rookie Biographies series.